Olga Popova

Psychology for Marketers

Olga Popova.

Psychology for Marketers
Astar.Marketing, 2025. — 64 p.
ISBN: 979-8-9940216-1-3

Illustrations — Tetiana Cherkashyna
Layout — Yuliia Sulima

This book is a practical guide—a clear, simple foundation for anyone who wants to quickly understand the psychology behind marketing and start applying it right away. There are no long theories here — only key principles, examples, and tools that genuinely work in business.
This is a roadmap that helps marketers support anyone who wants to understand clients better, see the whole picture, and act immediately.

Table of Contents

ABOUT THE AUTHOR

WHO IS OLGA POPOVA?

Olga Popova is a marketing strategist, educator, and author with over 20 years of hands-on experience helping businesses grow in competitive, fast-changing markets. She has worked with companies across the United States and Europe, supporting both local brands and international projects.

Olga specializes in digital marketing, brand positioning, marketing communications, and strategic development. She approaches marketing as an integrated system – from understanding customer psychology and defining a clear value proposition to launching campaigns, analyzing performance, and optimizing sales funnels. Her work focuses on building sustainable marketing strategies rather than chasing short-term trends.

Education is a core part of Olga's professional journey. She has taught marketing and digital strategy to students, entrepreneurs, and practicing professionals through academic programs, corporate training, and author-led courses. Her teaching style is practical and case-driven, emphasizing tools and frameworks that can be applied immediately in real business situations.

This book reflects Olga's belief that **effective marketing is rooted in psychology**, clarity, and ethical influence – not templates or buzzwords. Drawing on real-world experience, she explains how marketing truly works and how professionals can build systems that deliver long-term results.

Olga is currently based in the United States, where she runs her marketing agency, **Astar.Marketing**. She continues to develop educational content for marketers who want to move beyond "running ads" and instead create strong brands, meaningful customer relationships, and resilient marketing systems in digitally saturated markets.

How to Navigate This Book

This book is not a "magic pill," and it's not a collection of motivational quotes. It is a practical roadmap filled with checklists designed to help you see marketing from a fresh perspective. But here's the truth: if you simply flip through the pages, nothing will change.

Real results come when you:
- pause and revisit the key ideas;
- take the tools and test them in real situations;
- gradually build your own work habits around them.

I write concisely—with no fluff.
My first SMM course for business owners was called **"Effective SMM. No Fluff. Just Practice."** That's because I'm not an online "info-guru"; I am a hands-on marketer who works with real clients and real challenges. And that makes a difference.

So when I see countless "experts" promising to teach marketing in one month, it honestly makes me sad. I know the truth: that's an illusion—and I don't want that myth to keep spreading in the age of the internet.
The purpose of this book is simple: to show that marketing without psychology is only half the picture. When you begin to understand human behavior, motivations, and emotions, you start achieving a completely different level of results.
My advice: read slowly, revisit the important sections, take notes.
Try applying even a few techniques—and you will see change.
Not a dramatic "wow effect" in a week, but in two or three months you'll notice your strategy growing stronger and your business becoming more stable.

Part 1.
Psychological Foundations of Marketing Decisions

Why Does Marketing Need Psychology?

Many people think of marketing as advertising, SMM (Social Media Marketing), or sales. But marketing is much bigger than that.

At its core, marketing is the art of creating value and shaping the conditions that make decision-making easier.

A marketer's job is to help people see that their need can be met by a product or service — and to make that choice feel natural and safe. If the product doesn't seem useful, or if the company doesn't inspire trust, the sale simply won't happen.

What Is Psychology?

Psychology is the science of how people perceive the world, how they feel, think, and make decisions. It studies the internal mechanisms that drive the behavior of individuals and groups.
Marketing answers the question: "How do we deliver value and help a person choose?"

Psychology answers: "Why does a person make this choice?"
Without this understanding, marketers often work in the dark. They may get lucky sometimes — but they rarely build a consistent, reliable strategy.

Several Important Conclusions

• Do people's psychology and behavior change over time?
Our basic psychological needs — safety, love, belonging, recognition, and growth — have remained the same for thousands of years. What does change is our culture and the technologies we use.
Marketing communication evolves as new tools appear, but the internal triggers behind human decisions stay remarkably stable.

• Is psychology used in modern marketing?
Absolutely — and very actively.
Since the early 20th century, advertisers have experimented with headlines, visuals, colors, wording and messages to understand how these elements shape behavior. These early experiments laid the groundwork for today's marketing strategies.

• Do principles still work in the age of technology?
Yes. The tools may evolve, but the core principles remain unchanged.
Scarcity ("Only 2 items left"), social proof (reviews), authority (ratings), free trials — all of these rely on timeless psychological mechanisms.
Technology moves fast, but the human mind adapts slowly.

Five Reasons Marketers Need Psychology

1. *Understanding Motivation*

People don't buy a product — they buy the feeling or state it promises.
Shoes aren't just footwear; they represent comfort and confidence.
A car isn't only transportation; it symbolizes freedom and status.
When a marketer understands these deeper motives, they can craft messages that truly resonate.

2. *Capturing Attention*

Today people are hit with thousands of information signals every day.
The scarcest resource is no longer money — it is attention.
Psychology shows us how to catch the eye, spark curiosity, and stand out.
This can be done through contrasting colors, unusual shapes, emotional triggers, or even a simple question that interrupts someone's automatic scrolling.

3. *Shaping Perception of Value*

Price is always relative.
The same product can feel "too expensive" or "absolutely worth it," depending on the context.
Psychology explains key effects such as:

- **Anchoring** — the first number sets a mental benchmark.
- **Contrast effect** — people judge value by comparing options.
- **Choice framing** — decisions guided by "premium vs. basic" positioning.

4. *Social Influence*

We look to others for cues — often without realizing it.

When we see reviews, recommendations, or happy customers, we feel safer:

"If others tried – I can, too."
This is not pressure; it's natural human behavior shaped by our environment.

5. *Emotional Connection*

One purchase can be random.
Repeat purchases come from trust.
Strong, long-lasting businesses are built on emotional connection.
This is why brands invest in storytelling, community, and personalized service.
Customers return not just for the product – but for the feeling they ***associate*** with it.

Conclusion

Marketing without psychology is just guesswork.
You may occasionally guess right, but you can't build a stable, predictable system on luck.
When you combine marketing with psychology, you unlock a deeper level of understanding – not just how to influence decisions, but why those strategies work.
This is what allows businesses to become more resilient, sharpen their competitive edge, and build long-term relationships with their customers.

Psychology of Sales: Emotions and Decisions

What are sales?

From the buyer's perspective, sales are a journey — from recognizing a problem to choosing a solution. A person identifies a need, looks for options, compares prices and features, evaluates benefits, raises objections, and eventually makes a thoughtful decision.

From the marketer's perspective, sales are about creating the right conditions so the customer chooses our product over many others. And the goal isn't just a single transaction. What truly matters is that the customer is satisfied, comes back, and recommends the brand to others.

What drives successful sales?

Above all: **trust** and the removal of **mental barriers.**
People buy when doubts fade and value becomes clear.
This is where psychology becomes essential—because perception, emotion, and decision-making are psychological processes long before they are rational steps.

The Line Between Influence and Manipulation

People often call sales "pushing" or "imposing."

And yes, large corporations or governments can artificially shape demand through massive media pressure. But in small and medium-sized businesses, this almost always backfires. People sense dishonesty quickly, trust erodes, and reputation collapses. There is an unbreakable rule:

Even an average product will find a customer with competent, ethical marketing.

But if a customer feels deceived, repeat sales disappear — and reputation damage only grows.

Emotions vs. Logic

Is every sale manipulation?

No. Any influence – including sales – can be ethical or manipulative.

Human evolution has shaped the brain so that every stimulus is processed ***emotionally*** first and ***rationally*** second.
We feel before we think.

We justify our choices after we make them.
This is a universal mechanism; it works the same way for everyone.

Marketing works with this reality:
First – capture an emotion (trust, curiosity, excitement, a sense of value).
Then – support it with logic (features, terms, guarantees).
This is not dishonest if the product truly delivers value.

Just think about your own habits: impulse buys, first impressions, gut feelings, intuitive decisions that don't always fit "logic." These reactions are normal. Marketing simply uses natural psychological mechanisms that people already rely on.

Conclusion

Sales are not manipulation– they are **guided influence** built on a healthy balance of emotion and logic.
The difference lies in ethics:
If you help someone solve a problem – it is sales and value creation.
If you push something unnecessary by exploiting weaknesses – it's manipulation, and it eventually destroys the business.

Part 2.
Practical Psychomarketing Tools

Social Psychology in Marketing

Social psychology examines how people and groups shape our thoughts, emotions, and actions. For marketers, it's an essential tool. It helps explain why we often trust the opinions of complete strangers more than our own instincts, why an "expert recommendation" can outweigh pure logic, and why a simple countdown timer can push us to make decisions faster.

These behavioral patterns are rooted in human evolution, which is why they work everywhere — in retail stores, online shopping, and digital marketing. Robert Cialdini famously outlined these principles in his classic book ***"Influence: The Psychology of Persuasion."***

Robert Cialdini's 6 Principles of Influence

1. *Reciprocity*

How it works: *When someone gives us something, we naturally want to give something back.*

Examples:

- Beauty stores boost sales by handing out free samples.
- In B2B, offering checklists, whitepapers, or free consultations creates goodwill—and a subtle sense of obligation.
- Coca-Cola once gave out free drink vouchers during a promotion and saw sales jump by 20–30%.

2. *Commitment and Consistency*

How it works: *Once we take a small step, we're more likely to take the next one in order to stay consistent with our past behavior.*

Examples:

- Tripwire offers: buying a $7 mini-product makes customers more open to purchasing a $70 full course later.
- Free trials → subscription → purchase.
- Politics: "Sign this petition" → "Share this post" → deeper engagement and loyalty.

3. *Social Proof*

How it works: *When we're uncertain, we look at what other people are doing.*

Examples:

- Amazon's "Customers also bought..." section boosts trust and conversions.
- On Airbnb, reviews often matter more than the apartment description.
- On social media, likes, followers, and comments signal credibility.

4. *Liking (Affection)*

How it works: *We're more likely to trust people we like – or people who feel similar to us.*

Examples:

- Micro-influencers (10–50k followers) often drive higher conversions than big-name celebrities because they feel more relatable.
- UGC content – real client photos and videos – consistently outperforms polished ads.
- Small local businesses that show their real owners and team members build instant warmth and connection.

5. *Authority*

How it works: *We naturally trust experts, specialists, and people with recognized status.*

Examples:

- "Doctor-recommended" labels significantly boost credibility in healthcare and wellness products.
- Features in Forbes or speaking on a TEDx stage elevate perceived expertise.
- Established universities or long-standing institutions create stronger trust than newer, unknown schools.

6. Scarcity

How it works: *We're more motivated by the fear of missing out than by potential gains.*

Examples:

- E-commerce: "Only 2 items left in stock."
- Events: "Limited to 50 seats."
- Apple: long lines forming overnight.

Additional Effects in Marketing

Halo Effect

A *positive overall impression spills over onto everything else.*

Example: Tesla is viewed as innovative, so customers tend to overlook its flaws or quality issues.

Contrast Effect

We judge value by comparing one option with another.

Example: SaaS pricing tiers — placing a $199 plan next to a $29 plan makes the cheaper option feel like a steal.

Effort Justification

The more effort we put in, the more meaningful the outcome feels.

Example: 21-day challenges in fitness, learning, or productivity feel more valuable precisely because they require commitment.

Common Enemy Effect

A *shared "opponent" strengthens group identity and loyalty.*

Example: Brands that take a firm stance against plastic waste often build a devoted, eco-minded audience.

How The Brain Works in Marketing

- Attention triggers: Reciprocity, consistency, the halo effect, and even a shared "common enemy" all help grab attention in a crowded world.
- Value triggers: Scarcity, social proof, and effort justification make a product feel more valuable before the  customer even makes a decision.

- Social pressure: Authority, social proof, and consistency shape how people behave when they're uncertain — especially when they see how others act.
- Emotional triggers: Liking, the halo effect, and the common-enemy effect influence how people feel, which becomes the foundation for trust and long-term loyalty.

Conclusion

These principles aren't tricks or manipulation — they're natural parts of human psychology. Ignore them, and your marketing becomes guesswork. Use them ethically, and you build strong, lasting customer relationships.

Part 3.
Cognitive Biases in Marketing

What Are Cognitive Biases?

Cognitive biases are predictable thinking errors that lead us to make irrational decisions. They arise because the brain has limited time, energy, and information — so it relies on shortcuts called heuristics.

These mental shortcuts were studied and described by Daniel Kahneman, Amos Tversky, and later Dan Ariely.

For marketers, understanding these patterns is like discovering a treasure map: biases help you anticipate how customers think, choose, and behave.

Most Common Cognitive Biases in Marketing

1. *Fundamental Attribution Error*

We attribute our own behavior to our personal qualities – but blame other people's behavior on circumstances.

Examples:

- "I bought the premium model because I value quality."
- "He bought it only because it was on sale."

In marketing:

- Premium products are sold by appealing to identity: "You deserve the best."
- Mass-market promotions lean on situational framing: "Flash sale – don't miss it."

2. *Confirmation Bias*

We actively look for information that supports what we already believe – and ignore anything that challenges it.

In marketing:

- On marketplaces, shoppers search for reviews that confirm their first impression.
- Claims like "96% of customers recommend this" feed confirmation bias instantly.

3. Optimism Bias

We overestimate the likelihood of positive events and underestimate risks.

Examples:

- "I won't get into an accident."
- "This subscription will definitely pay off."

In marketing:

- Insurance upsells: "Basic is enough" → the person downplays the risks.
- Fitness programs: "You'll get results faster" → reinforces the natural tendency to expect the best.

4. Framing Effect

The way information is framed completely changes how we interpret it.

Examples:

- "95% success rate" feels much better than "5% failure."
- "Only $1 per day" feels lighter than "$365 per year."

In marketing:

- Netflix: "Only $9.99 per month."
- FMCG: "Under 100 calories per serving" instead of "20 grams of sugar."

5. Hindsight Bias

After something happens, we convince ourselves we "knew it all along."

Example:

- "I felt it was the right choice."

In marketing:

- Testimonials: "I always knew this course would transform my career."
- Loyalty programs: "I've been with you for years – it's always been the right choice."

6. *Clip Thinking*

Today, attention comes in quick, fragmented bursts. The first seconds matter the most.

Examples:

- TikTok/Reels: you have 3–5 seconds to hook someone.
- Endless scrolling: you train your brain to expect constant novelty.
- Dopamine loop: "one more video ... one more click."

In marketing:

- On YouTube, the first 5 seconds of an ad decide whether the viewer stays or skips.
- Strong visual hooks and emotional reactions outperform slow intros.
- Promo formulas work best when they follow a simple pattern: short hook + meaningful message.
-

Simple rule: a quick hook opens the door – deeper meaning keeps the person inside.

How Marketing Uses Cognitive Biases

1. *Understanding Needs and Motivation*

- Framing helps you show the product in the best possible light.
- Hindsight bias strengthens the customer's belief that they made the right choice.

Example:

Apple doesn't sell the iPhone as "just a smartphone" — it sells a lifestyle.

2. *Attracting Attention*

- Framing lets you test different versions of the same message to see which angle resonates most.

3. *Managing Price Perception*

- Framing can turn a price into a "small, manageable expense."
- The contrast effect makes high prices feel normal — and lower prices feel like a deal.

Example:

SaaS pricing tiers: Pro $199 vs. Basic $29 → the Basic plan suddenly looks very reasonable.

4. *Using Social Norms and Pressure*

- Optimism bias makes people believe in the best-case sccnarioapplics to thcm.
- Hindsight bias helps them feel they "always knew" they were making the right decision.

Example:

Booking.com: “14 people are viewing this hotel right now.”

5. *Creating Emotional Connection*

- Optimism bias builds the expectation that the next purchase or experience will be even better.
- Hindsight bias helps people rationalize emotional decisions, making them feel intentional and smart.

Example:

Spotify’s personalized playlists → users feel: “This service really gets me.”

Conclusion

Cognitive biases aren’t flaws – they’re evolutionary tools that help the brain make decisions quickly in uncertain situations.
Marketing uses these mechanisms to clarify value, highlight meaning, and build trust.
But one rule always applies: **influence ≠ manipulation.**
Ethical marketing uses psychological insights to help customers make good decisions – not to deceive them.

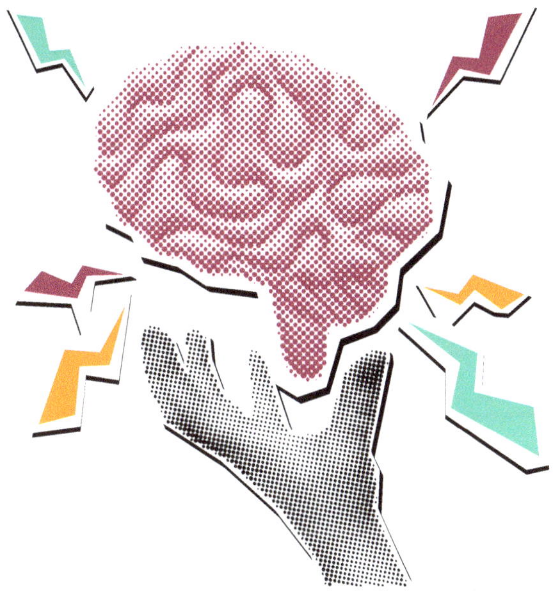

Part 4.
Language of Influence in Marketing

What Is NLP Really and Is It Worth Mentioning?

Marketing has used subconscious influence techniques for decades. Some come from NLP, others from cognitive psychology and classic advertising research.
Neuro-linguistic programming (NLP) is a set of models and techniques that describe how people perceive reality, organize their experiences, and make decisions. Created in the 1970s by Richard Bandler and John Grinder, NLP grew out of studying the language and behavior of therapists, advertisers, and influential communicators.

Their main discovery:
language and nonverbal cues can shift a person's internal state.

In marketing, NLP became popular because it offers practical tools for:

- building trust;
- increasing motivation;
- removing objections;
- shaping behavior through words and imagery.

Myth: "NLP is mind control."

Reality: NLP is simply a set of communication techniques based on how our thinking and perception naturally work.

How does NLP work in marketing?

1. People think in images and sensations, not words. Language only triggers internal images. When advertising activates the needed image – "the taste of childhood," "the feeling of freedom" – it instantly becomes more persuasive.

2. The brain avoids overload.
   We skim information and rely on associations and emotions. NLP provides tools to enhance those associations.

3. Communication always happens on two levels: the conscious (logic) and the subconscious (emotions and imagery). Marketing that speaks to both levels at once is the most effective.

NLP Techniques in Marketing Communications

1. *Appeal to identity*

When a product speaks directly to who a person believes they are.

Examples:

- Harley-Davidson: "You're not just buying a bike – you're joining a brotherhood."
- Apple: "Think Different" – a message built for "the select few," people who see themselves as creative and unique.

2. *Hierarchy of values*

Every person has their individual "value compass": freedom, love, health, safety, success.

Examples:

- Airbnb: "Belong Anywhere" – appeals to the value of home and safety.
- L'Oréal: "Because you're worth it" – appeals to self-worth and confidence.

3. *Awakening emotions*

- Marketing works by awakening key emotions.
- Positive emotions: hope, anticipation, love.
- Negative emotions: fear, loneliness, disgust (used carefully and ethically).

Examples:

- Coca-Cola: "Open Happiness" → evokes joy and togetherness.
- Insurance campaigns: "protect your family" → tap into fear of loss to highlight responsibility and safety.

4. *Motivational promises*

Selling the transformation, not just the product.

Examples:

- English courses: “Speak freely with anyone in the world.”
- Fitness programs: “A new life without insecurities.”

Important: Big promises require real proof — case studies, reviews, and authentic success stories — or they damage trust.

5. *Open-ended questions*

These questions pull a person into the decision-making process and help shape their thinking.

Examples:

- “What matters more to you — speed or reliability?”
- The customer defines their own criteria, and your product can then be positioned to match them.

6. *Rhetorical questions*

A subtle way to guide perception by suggesting an answer without forcing it.

Examples:

- “Don’t you deserve more?”
- “Coincidence? I don’t think so!” — a classic line that plants the reaction you want without inviting debate.

7. *Objection reframing*

Addressing concerns before the customer brings them up.

Examples:

- Car dealership: "Worried about gas mileage? This model cuts fuel use by 20%."
- SaaS: "Think it's complicated? Most users learn it in under 30 minutes."

Theoretical Background and Criticism

- NLP is often criticized for lacking a strong scientific foundation. Indeed, many of its techniques haven't been validated through academic research.
- Yet in practical marketing, many of these methods still work — because they tap into how people naturally think: cognitive shortcuts, emotional triggers, and familiar decision-making patterns.
- Today, NLP-inspired tools show up everywhere: copywriting, storytelling, sales funnels, and the customer journey.

Conclusion

The language of influence in marketing isn't a "magic sales button," but a set of tools that blends psychology, communication, and marketing.

- It helps you speak to a customer's identity, values, emotions, and hidden objections.
- And it must be used ethically - supporting informed decisions, not manipulating them.

When marketers master these tools, they gain real insight into subconscious decision-making and can create messaging that builds trust and long-term relationships.

Part 5.
Timeless Psychological Techniques That Always Work

Marketing draws from countless theories, studies, and frameworks. But there's another category – practical methods that have stood the test of time. These techniques run so deep in human culture and psychology that they work almost everywhere, no matter the country, generation, or industry.

They're "timeless" because they tap into universal human instincts:

- the drive to survive,
- the need to belong,

• the desire for a better future,
• the wish to be recognized,
• and the fear of missing out or losing something valuable.

In this chapter, I've gathered the tools that consistently deliver results — both in my own work and in the work of countless marketers.

1. *Show the Consequences (Fear of Loss)*

People are far more motivated by avoiding loss than by chasing gains. This isn't guesswork — it's one of the most documented principles in psychology.

Example:

Insurance ads rarely sell "a policy." Instead, they show a moment of crisis — a crash, a hospital room, a family in shock — followed by the message: "This could have been prevented."

In the digital world, SaaS brands use the same logic:

"Without our CRM, you're losing up to 20% of potential customers every month."

Suddenly the abstract becomes real — the customer can see the loss.

2. *Quotes and Authorities*

Appeals to authority work especially well for people who rely on "external signals" when making decisions. They want validation from a trusted expert or a recognizable leader.

Examples:

- Nike partners with world champions to instantly boost credibility.
- TED built an entire brand around "ideas worth spreading," using scientists and thought leaders as social proof.

- Even a small business can borrow authority – a timely quote from a respected figure can dramatically strengthen a message.

3. *Compliments and Flattery*

Compliments aren't just for the naive – they work on everyone. People want to feel seen, valued, and appreciated.
The trick is subtlety. Flattery is like seasoning: a little brings out the flavor; too much overwhelms the dish.

Example:

Amazon often opens emails with lines like, "You're one of our most valued customers." Of course, thousands receive the same message – but each person still feels recognized.

4. *Exclusivity and Belonging to the Elite*

The desire to feel "chosen" runs deep. People love being part of something exclusive – a club, a tribe, an inner circle.

Examples:

- Apple built an entire culture around the iPhone: you're not just buying a device – you're joining a community.
- Louis Vuitton or Rolex reinforce status through VIP programs and limited-access experiences.
- Online courses do the same with "premium tiers" and members-only perks.

5. *Temptation and Teasing*

Human behavior always moves from discomfort to relief, from tension to satisfaction. A marketer's job is to create that emotional arc.

Example:

A coffee ad might start with: "*Another sluggish morning?*"
Then resolve it with: "*One cup, and everything clicks into place.*"

The key is temptation, not full disclosure. If you show everything upfront, the intrigue disappears – and so does the desire.

6. Secrets and "Forgotten Knowledge"

People can't resist unfinished stories. This is the Zeigarnik effect: when something feels incomplete, we naturally want to return to it.

Examples:

- Netflix keeps audiences hooked with expertly timed cliffhangers.
- Marketers often use: "We'll reveal the secret only after you sign up."
- But the rule is simple: if you promise a secret, you absolutely must deliver. Break that promise once, and trust collapses.

7. Subtext

Direct claims often feel forced or unbelievable. Subtext – letting the customer draw their own conclusions – is far more powerful.

Example: Saying, "*I'm rich,*" *sounds fake.*
But: "*Yesterday my bank manager called to congratulate me – my deposit just passed $1 million,*" lets the listener connect the dots themselves.

Subtext builds authenticity where direct statements fall flat.

8. Magic and Sense of Mystery

Products with a backstory or legend carry an aura of magic. That sense of mystery adds perceived value.

Examples:

- Rolex: "A watch built to outlast generations."
- Car brands love referencing aviation or military heritage — it makes the technology feel almost mythical.

9. *The Challenge ("Show Us What You've Got")*

A challenge triggers a natural human response: the urge to prove yourself.

Examples:

- Nike: "Think you can't? Just Do It."
- Online courses: "Most people never finish. Will you be the exception?"
-

When framed correctly, a challenge taps into pride, competitiveness, and personal growth.

10. *"This is your idea"*

People rarely push back against their own decisions.

If a customer arrives at the conclusion themselves, the sale is practically done.

Example:

A salesperson leads with a few simple questions — three quick "yeses" — and the customer eventually says:
"So I *guess I really do need this.*"
When the idea feels self-generated, resistance drops to zero.

11. *The Guilt Trigger*

A powerful, but risky technique.
It taps into the feeling of "I should be doing more."

Examples:

- Charities: "Can't you give just $1 to help save a child's life?"
- Courses: "If you truly wanted change, wouldn't you have started already?"

12. *Promising a Life Change*

People don't buy products – they buy transformation.
A better life. A better version of themselves.

Example:

- "In 90 days, you'll transform your body — and your life."
- MLM pitch::"This opportunity will finally change your destiny."

These messages work because they sell a narrative of personal reinvention.

13. *No Alternatives*

Positioning your offer as the only real solution creates urgency and confidence – sometimes too much of it.

Examples:

- Apple positioned iOS as the "only right" ecosystem.
- SaaS brands often claim: "Top companies already trust us — there's no better option."

This technique works, but only when the product truly delivers on that promise.

Conclusion

These aren't "tricks" — they're psychological fundamentals. They work because they tap into core human drives:

- fear of loss,
- the need to belong,
- the desire for recognition,
- the dreams of personal transformation.

The key is balance.
The right dose makes your marketing persuasive and compelling. Overuse turns it into manipulation — and customers will run the other way.

Part 6.
What Is Copywriting Through the Lens of Psychology?

In early 20th-century America, the words copywriting, marketing, and advertising were often used interchangeably – and for good reason.

Marketing revolved around advertising, and advertising was overwhelmingly text-based: newspapers, magazines, flyers, direct mail.

Human civilization is built on writing. Text allowed us to pass knowledge, survival strategies, and culture across time and distance. Without writing, we'd still be limited to small groups and oral storytelling.
Writing breaks barriers.

Copywriting is simply selling through text at a distance.

And text integrates every psychological principle we've discussed:

- It uncovers needs and motivations.
- It captures attention.
- It reframes price and removes objections.
- It incorporates social proof.
- It builds emotional connection.

In other words: **good copy replaces a salesperson.**
Unlike a salesperson, though, text works 24/7.

It doesn't take breaks, doesn't get sick, and doesn't ask for a raise. A single well-crafted piece of copy can deliver results for months – even years.

Even in the age of TikTok and video-first platforms, text remains the backbone of communication.
Just look at the rise of newsletter platforms and Telegram channels — at the core, it's still all about words.

Copywriting as a Psychological Tool

Why is text so powerful?
Because it speaks directly to our psychology.

- Words as Light Hypnosis

Great copy is a form of gentle persuasion — almost like light hypnosis.
Its job is to slip past our critical filters and create a "yes-ready" mindset.
How?
By distracting the conscious mind and speaking to emotions.
A reader gets a few paragraphs in and suddenly feels:

"You know what... this might be worth trying."

- The BrainIs Lazy — by Design

Our brain is incredibly energy-intensive. During deep thinking, it uses up to 25% of the body's energy.
To conserve energy, the mind relies on shortcuts: heuristics, biases, and fast-thinking patterns.
Copywriting works with these switches.
When the brain feels overloaded or tired, it defaults to automatic decision-making — and persuasive text guides that automatic mode.

- Emotion First, Logic Second

Effective copy triggers emotion first — fear of missing out, hope, curiosity, belonging — and only then introduces rational proof (features, benefits, guarantees).

This isn't manipulation; it's biology. Humans feel first and reason second.

Why Copywriting Works?

Emotional spark → logical justification → objection removal.

Examples:

Google Ads test:

- "CRM for business" → CTR: 1.2%
- "Losing customers? Try CRM for free" → CTR: 3.1%

Same budget, triple the clicks – because emotion wins.

Email marketing: In the mailshots of a chain of coffee shops:

- "20% discount this Friday" → 14% open rate
- "Your favorite coffee is waiting for you tomorrow" → 29% open rate

Emotional personalization doubled opens.

Copywriting isn't just putting words together.

It's a psychological technology of influence – structured, strategic, and deeply human.

AI as the New Copywriter

A new player has entered the field – artificial intelligence. What once required a trained copywriter is now accessible to anyone using tools like ChatGPT, Claude, Jasper, and Copy.ai.

- **Spccd.**

AI produces text instantly.

What used to take hours — articles, social ads, landing pages — now takes minutes.

- **Scale.**

AI can draft hundreds of headlines, CTAs, product descriptions, or ad variations and help test them at scale.

- **Adaptability.**

It adjusts tone and style effortlessly: formal business, playful Instagram captions, CEO-level thought leadership — anything.

But Here's the Catch.
AI still doesn't truly feel human psychology.
It recognizes patterns in words, not in emotions.
It can imitate emotional language, but it doesn't instinctively sense what sparks desire, fear, trust, or curiosity.
That's where the human comes in.

The New Formula
AI + marketing psychologist = unbeatable copywriting.

AI handles the output.
The marketer handles the insight — the motivations, fears, triggers, decision-making patterns.
Together, they create copy that is fast and deeply persuasive.

Conclusion

We examined three core pillars of modern marketing: strategy, sales, and copywriting.

- Marketing creates value and shapes demand.
- Sales convert interest into action.
- Copywriting is the language that keeps the conversation going with the customer.

In the 20th century, copywriting was a craft reserved for a small circle of professionals.

In the 21st, with the rise of AI, it has become a widely accessible tool — something anyone can use.

But one truth hasn't changed: good copywriting is psychology in action.

If you want to truly master marketing, you need to understand people — their emotions, their motivations, and how they think. Because copy only works when it speaks the language of the customer's subconscious.

Part 7.
The Psychology Behind a Marketer's Success: How to Break Through Limitations and Stay Grounded

A Marketer Between Two Worlds

At first glance, marketing looks glamorous – presentations, videos, campaigns, constant creativity.
But behind that polished surface are late nights, endless revisions, tight deadlines, and clients who needed everything "yesterday."
A marketer exists in two parallel worlds:
one driven by numbers, analytics, and KPIs, the other driven by human emotions, wants, and fears.
Balancing these two forces is the heart of the profession.
And psychology becomes the foundation – the only way to understand the client while also surviving the pressure that comes with the job.

The Invisible Ceiling

Every professional eventually runs into an "invisible ceiling."
You know your craft, you outperform many around you – yet something keeps holding you back.
You watch colleagues land bigger clients, earn more, or join global teams, and you can't help but wonder:
"Why are they there and I'm still here?"
The causes vary:

- limiting beliefs ("Success isn't for people like me"),
- fear of failure,
- or simple burnout and exhaustion.

This ceiling isn't external — it's psychological.

The Psychology of Money and Ambition

To grow — and to sustain that growth — a marketer needs four things:

- **Passion.** The work should excite you from the inside.
- **Ambition.** Your goals should always be slightly beyond your current abilities.
- **Mission.** Your projects should matter — not just pay.
- **Discipline.** Show up consistently, even when inspiration doesn't.

According to Glassdoor (2024):
In the U.S., the average salary for a digital marketing manager is about **$78,000 per year.**
In Europe, it's around **€45,000.**
In Ukraine, it ranges from **₴90,000–120,000 per month.**

The gap isn't just about money — it reflects the demands, the level of responsibility, and the mindset expected from specialists in different markets.

Marketer and Stress:

The Hidden Cost of the Profession

Marketing is one of the most stressful careers out there.
Marketers work as a constant "buffer" between clients, leadership, and their own team.
It's like being a conductor whose orchestra is playing three different songs at once: the client wants one thing, leadership wants another, the team is overwhelmed, and the market changes by the day.

HubSpot, 2023: 63% of U.S. marketers report high stress every week, and 41% say they're close to burnout.

CMO *Council*, 2024: In Europe, 56% of marketers say their job has negatively impacted their health, and nearly one-third are considering leaving the profession entirely.

DOU.*ua*, 2024: In Ukraine, stress levels spiked after 2022 as most marketers shifted to remote work and began juggling multiple clients at once.

What Burnout Looks Like

It starts as simple fatigue.
Then even your most successful campaigns don't feel satisfying anymore.
Next comes irritation — every edit, every message, every task feels heavy.
And eventually, you hit indifference.
Christina Maslach's classic burnout model outlines three stages:

1. **Emotional exhaustion.** A deep, constant tiredness that doesn't disappear — even after days off.
2. **Depersonalization.** Clients and colleagues start to feel like burdens rather than people.
3. **Loss of meaning.** Work becomes purely mechanical — just checking boxes.

How to Protect Yourself

In marketing, the people who last the longest aren't the ones who work the hardest — but the ones who know how to recover.

What actually helps:

- **Clear boundaries:** set expectations for communication and working hours.

- **Delegation:** you don't have to (and shouldn't) carry everything yourself.
- **Therapy or coaching:** a professional investment, not a weakness.
- **Exercise and meditation:** they reset your attention and conserve energy.
- **Rest:** sometimes the smartest move is stepping back so you can return stronger.

APA, 2022: After 10 therapy sessions, 68% of creative-industry professionals reported lower anxiety and renewed energy.

Effective Self-Help Practices for Marketers

1. *The "3-3-3 Rule"*

Name three objects around you, touch three surfaces, take three slow breaths.
This helps ground you and reduces anxiety.

2. *Pomodoro + Reset*

Work for 25 minutes, break for 5.
After four cycles, take a 15-minute deep rest.
Your brain handles pressure better in structured blocks.

3. *Digital Detox*

No screens for at least an hour before bed.
Set "Do Not Disturb" starting at 9 p.m.
This lowers cortisol and improves sleep quality.

4. *Two-Minute Micro-Meditations*

Close your eyes, focus on breathing:
inhale for 4 seconds → exhale for 6 seconds.
A quick energy reset between meetings.

5. *Physical Anchors*

20-minute daily walk + two workouts per week.
Movement is the simplest way to burn off stress hormones.

6. *Morning Body Scan*

Mentally scan your body from feet to head, notice tension, and release it.
Great for catching "hidden" fatigue.

7. *Emotion Journal*

Each day, write down:

- What inspired you,

- What drained you,

- What you are grateful for.

After a month, patterns become emerge — what fuels you and what drains you.

8. *The STOP Technique*

Stop → Take a breath → Observe → Proceed.
Use it before tough conversations or negotiations.

9. *Mini-rituals of Recovery*

A cup of tea without your phone.
A short walk after finishing a project.
A small reward at the end of a long day.
These simple rituals help you maintain long-term energy and prevent burnout from building up quietly in the background.

10. Psychotherapy and Coaching

Working with a therapist or coach isn't a luxury — it's a career investment.
And professional communities like the American Marketing Association (AMA) or local marketing groups offer support, mentorship, and a sense of belonging that's essential in a high-pressure field.

AI in Marketing:

Between Algorithms and Trust

Over the past few years, marketers have faced a new kind of challenge — artificial intelligence.
AI can write text, generate images, pull insights from data, and run calculations faster than any human. This saves enormous amounts of time...
but also creates the uneasy feeling that the profession might vanish.

Algorithms as a "Dopamine Machine"

AI churns out content designed to trigger quick bursts of satisfaction.
The cycle becomes addictive: new video → dopamine → "one more click."
The result?
People get used to reacting quickly but superficially.
For marketers, this means **attention is harder to capture and stress levels climb** as the race for engagement speeds up.

Marketers' Fears

With tools like ChatGPT, MidJourney, and countless automation platforms, many marketers quietly wondered:

"Am I still needed?"

But here's the truth:
AI can automate tasks, but it cannot understand context.
It can imitate emotion, but it does not feel.
It can generate content, but it cannot create trust.

AI isn't the end of marketing – **it's the next level of the game.**

Those who rely on copy-paste prompts may indeed become replaceable.
But those who understand **human psychology** and use AI as a strategic tool will pull ahead.

The Task of the Future Marketer

To stay relevant, a marketer must become the bridge between machines and people – protecting trust, empathy, and meaning in places where algorithms see only numbers and patterns.

Conclusion

Marketing is a field of tremendous opportunity and equally significant risk.
It offers freedom, high earning potential, and the ability to shape culture and influence industries.
But it also consumes energy, tests emotional endurance, and challenges mental resilience.
Being a marketer means learning not only to craft stories for your audience, but also to protect the story you're living yourself.

Success comes not just from skills and knowledge, but from safeguarding the human being behind the work — the part of you that dreams, feels joy, and wants a meaningful life.

Marketing is not only about strategies, tools, or budgets.
It's about people — their emotions, needs, fears, and hopes.
And to understand others, you must first understand yourself.

For a marketer, studying psychology isn't optional — it's essential.
It's the foundation of strong brands, honest communication, and resilience under pressure.

Therapy, coaching, and self-reflection aren't signs of weakness.
They're professional resources.
The better you understand your own motivation and stress patterns, the more effectively you can work with clients, teammates, and audiences.

There's one truth you rarely see in marketing textbooks:
Protect yourself.
Don't work with people who drain you or erode your confidence.

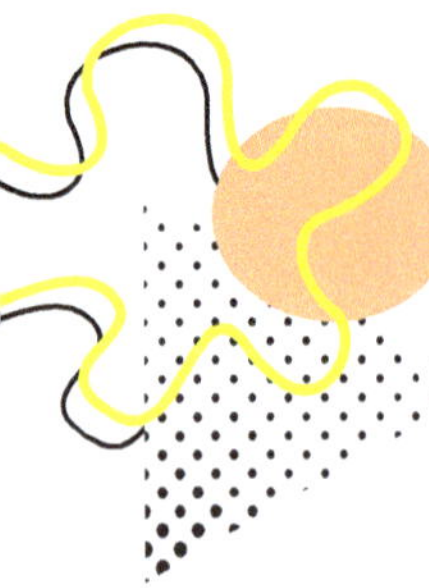

There will always be more clients and more projects — but there is only one you.

No fee is worth losing health or your self-respect.

Real value lies not in how many campaigns you've run, but in your ability to combine professionalism with balance.

Great marketing begins with the inner balance of the person who creates it.

Part 8.
Working Materials

This chapter brings together practical, ready-to-use tools for your daily work as a marketer.
It's divided into three parts:

1. **Checklists** – quick-reference guides for everyday marketing tasks and campaign prep.
2. **Schemes** – visual frameworks that help you clarify ideas and explain them to your team.
3. **Recommended Reading** – a curated list of books to deepen your understanding of marketing and psychology.

Use the **checklists** as your go-to reminders before launching or optimizing any campaign.

Review the **schemes** when you need to see the bigger picture or communicate a concept clearly.

Turn to the **reading list** whenever you want to reinforce your practical skills with solid theory.

Appendices

CHECKLISTS

1. Psychological Foundations of Marketing Decisions

- Do we clearly understand the customer's motivation?
- Is there an emotional hook in the message?
- Does the brand inspire trust?

- Are we accounting for attention biases (what naturally draws the customer's eye)?
- Have we created an emotional connection that supports repeat purchases?
- Does the product truly match the customer's needs?

2. *Psychomarketing Tools (Cialdini's Principles)*

- Are core influence principles applied (reciprocity, consistency, social proof, liking, authority, scarcity)?
- Is scarcity real — not manufactured?
- Is there a strong emotional component (likability, halo effect, shared values, common enemy)?
- Have multiple message formats been tested?

3. *Cognitive Biases in Marketing*

- Is framing used effectively (positive vs. negative contrast)?
- Is social proof present (reviews, ratings, case studies)?
- Do we consider that different audience segments respond to biases differently?
- Is the anchoring effect used (initial price or number as a reference point)?

4. *The Language of Influence (Logic + Emotion)*

- Does the message speak to identity ("This is who I am / the group I belong to")?
- Are core values highlighted (success, safety, freedom, meaning)?

5. *Timeless Psychological Techniques*

- Is the fear-of-loss effect used?
- Is there social proof or an authority quote?
- Is there intrigue or mystery?
- Does the message create a sense of belonging?
- Does the customer feel valued and recognized?
- Are we using these techniques ethically and in moderation?

6. *Copywriting as a Psychological Tool*

- Does the headline spark emotion?
- Does the copy address objections?
- Is there a story or short narrative thread?
- Is there a real call-to-action?
- Is the text easy to read (structure, claritiy, spacing)?
- Does the tone match the target audience?

7. *Psychology of a Marketer's Success*

- Are personal boundaries clearly set?
- Is there a healthy work–rest balance?
- Are you building stress resilience (exercise, therapy, breaks)?
- Is there a recovery system in place (hobbies, environment, rest routines)?
- Are you protecting your internal resources?
- Do you feel meaning and mission in your work?

SCHEMES

1.
Customer Journey:
Stages and Psychological Triggers

A roadmap showing the customer's path from problem awareness to repeat purchase – and the key psychological drivers at each stage:

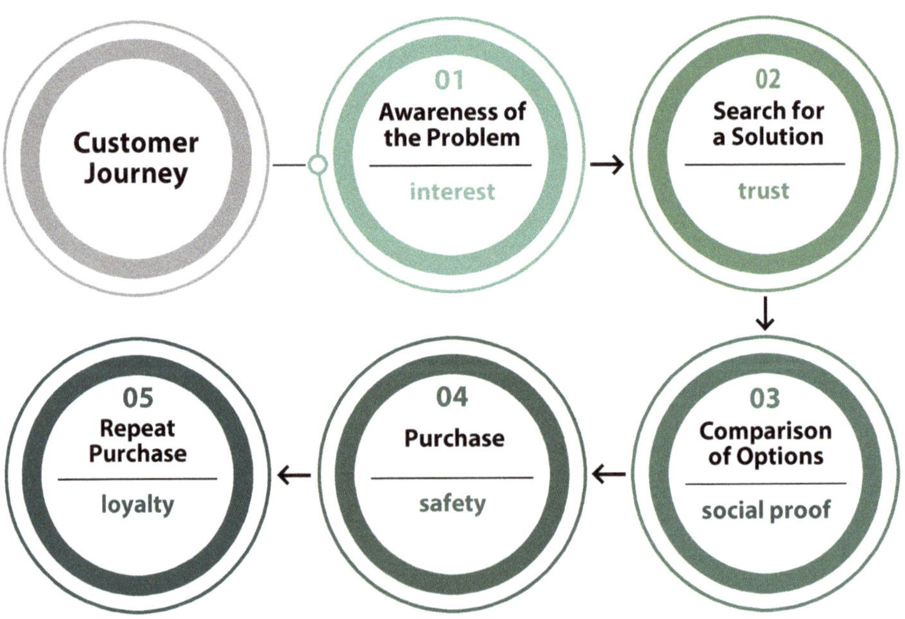

2.

Cialdini's 6 Principles of Influence

Six universal principles of persuasion that work across industries:

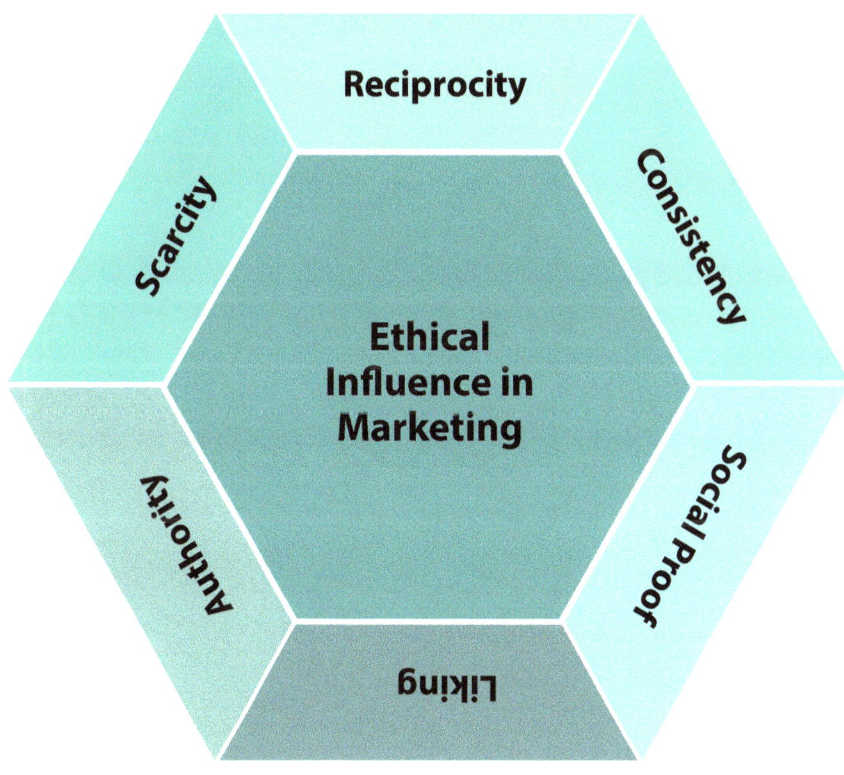

Infographic: six core principles of persuasion

3.

The Brain in Traps: Cognitive Biases

A visual map of the most common cognitive distortions shaping consumer behavior:

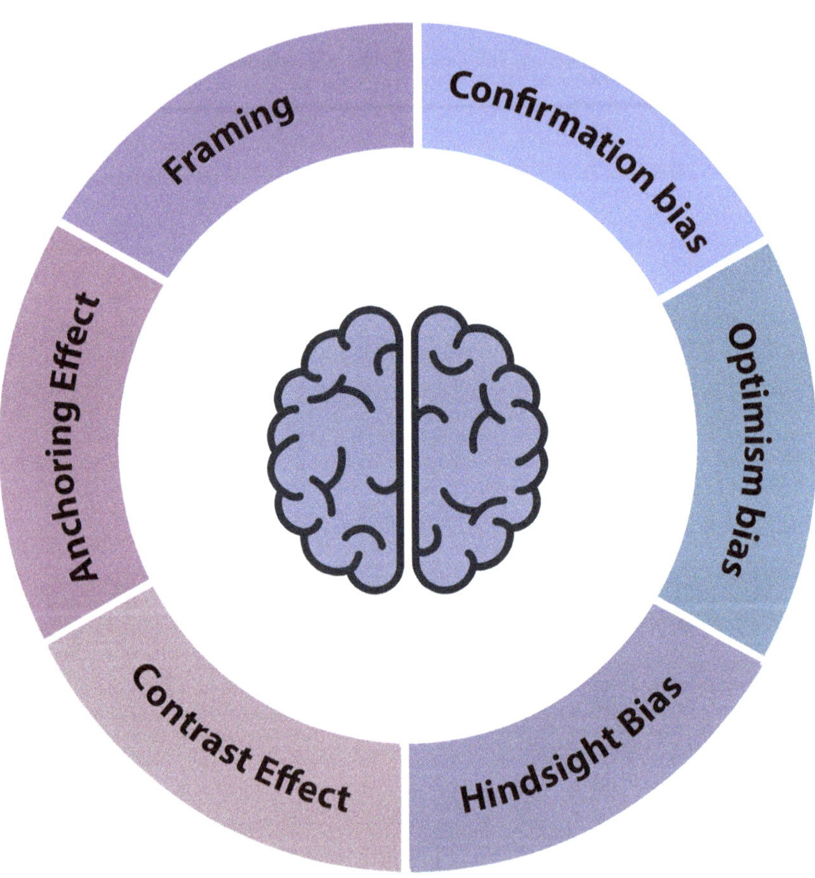

A visual map of the most common cognitive distortions shaping consumer behavior: Framing, Confirmation Bias, Optimism Bias, Hindsight Bias, Contrast Effect, Anchoring Effect

4.

The Language of Influence: Dual Channel

Two communication channels — logic and emotion — meet at the point of decision-making.

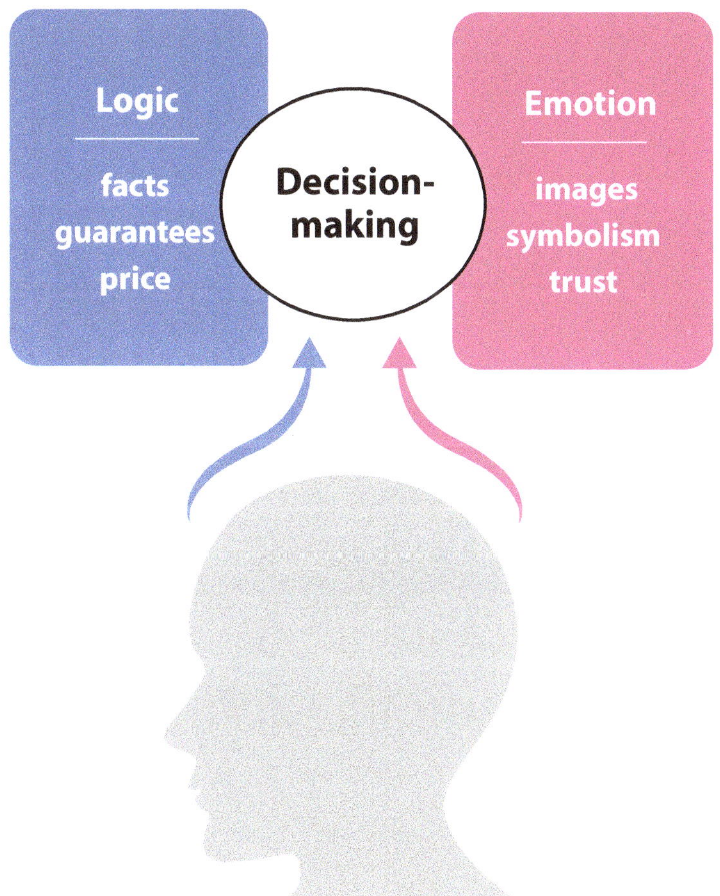

Two communication channels — logic and emotion — meet at the point of decision-making. Logic: facts, guarantees, price. Emotion: images, symbolism, trust. A strong message balances both.

5.

Twelve Timeless Psychological Triggers

A circle of 12 deep-rooted human motivators:

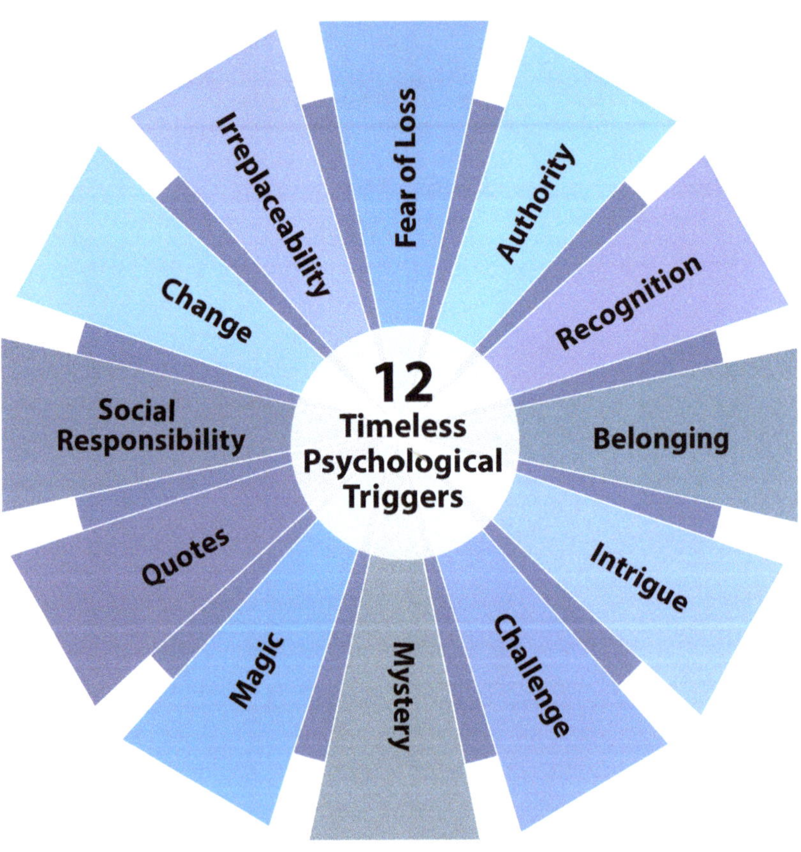

A circle of 12 deep-rooted human motivators:
Fear of Loss, Authority, Recognition, Belonging, Intrigue, Challenge, Mystery, Magic, Quotes, Social Responsibility, Change, Irreplaceability

6.

The Formula for a High-Conversion Text

The essential sequence behind persuasive copy:

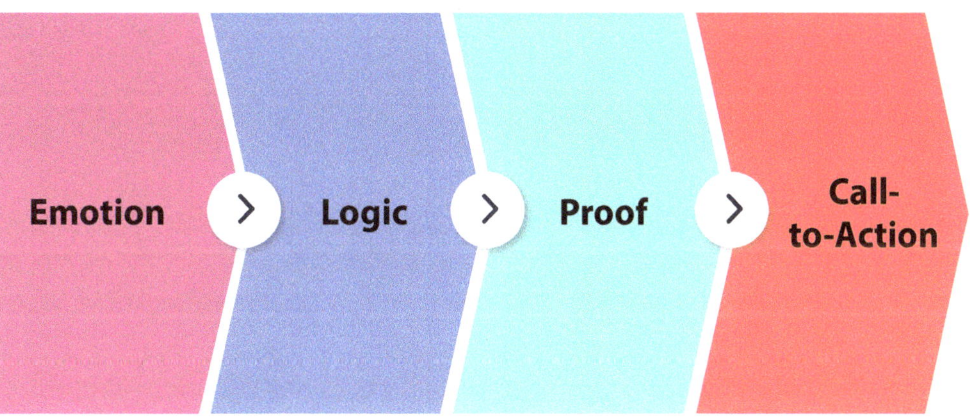

Emotion opens the door. Logic reinforces.
Proof builds trust. The CTA activates the decision

7.

Balance of a marketer's profession

The Balance of a Marketer's Work.
A psychological balance between effectiveness and personal well-being.

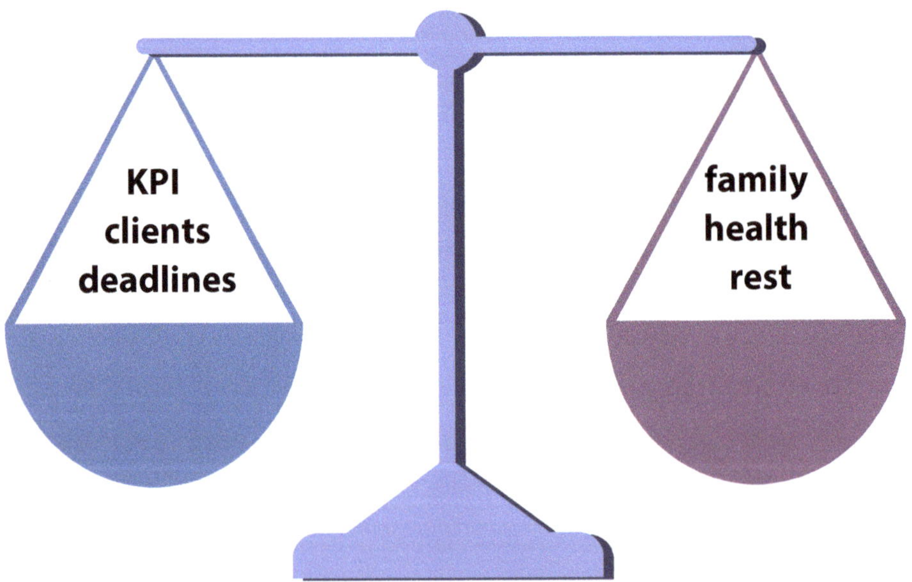

Without balance, even your best campaigns eventually drain you.

Recommended Literature

Recommended Reading

- **Robert Cialdini — *Influence: The Psychology of Persuasion***
  The classic on the six principles of influence: reciprocity, consistency, social proof, liking, authority, scarcity.

- **Daniel Kahneman — *Thinking, Fast and Slow***
  A Nobel laureate explains how fast and slow thinking shape decisions.

- **Christina Maslach, Michael Leiter — *The Truth About Burnout***
  A foundational guide to burnout: what causes it, how it develops, and how to prevent it.

- **Steven Levitt, Stephen Dubner — *Freakonomics***
  A fresh look at hidden behavioral patterns and surprising economic logic in everyday life.

- **Seth Godin — *This Is Marketing***
  A modern view of marketing as the art of creating meaningful change.

- **Chip Heath, Dan Heath — *Made to Stick***
  A practical guide to crafting memorable, high-impact ideas.

- **David Aaker — *Building Strong Brands***
  A foundational guide to building powerful brands and sustaining their long-term growth in competitive markets.

- **Malcolm Gladwell – *The Tipping Point***
  An exploration of how small shifts can spark major social change and lead to breakthrough moments.

- **Brené Brown – *Dare to Lead***
  A compelling perspective on leadership rooted in vulnerability, courage, and empathy. Especially valuable for managers and marketers working with teams.

Let's keep in touch

This book is just the beginning of the conversation.
More stories, real-world examples, practical tools, and answers to the questions marketers often "save for later" are still ahead.

You're welcome to connect with me here:

LinkedIn : https://www.linkedin.com/in/pani-olga-popova — My professional space, where I share insights, experience, and reflections from the marketing world.

Facebook: https://www.facebook.com/popova.kharkov — A more personal channel with updates, announcements, and open conversation.

On Facebook, you're welcome to message me directly — ask questions, share your thoughts, or tell me how the ideas from this book have supported your work.

One small note: I respond only to real people — real names, real photos. No empty profiles or bots.

Marketing has always been about community and shared experience.

So connect, reach out, and let's keep the dialogue going.